D1479947

Travel Across America

COLOR BY NUMBER

8   16   24   3   18   5

COLORING BOOK

ILLUSTRATED BY DEBRA GABEL

Debra Gabel, (designer, quilter, lecturer, author, fiber artist, business professional) started teaching and patterning quilts in 2000. Debra teaches and lectures internationally at quilt guilds, seminars, and fiber events. She aims to travel the world through quilting.
zebrapatterns.com

 **PUBLISHING ctpub.com**   P.O. Box 1456 • Lafayette, CA 94549 • 800.284.1114   Copyright © 2017 by Debra Gabel. All rights reserved.

STATE	flower	bird
ALABAMA	Camellia	Yellowhammer
ALASKA	Forget-me-not	Willow Ptarmigan
ARIZONA	Saguaro cactus blossom	Cactus Wren
ARKANSAS	Apple blossom	Mockingbird
CALIFORNIA	California poppy	California Valley Quail
COLORADO	Rocky Mountain Columbine	Lark Bunting
CONNECTICUT	Mountain laurel	Robin
DELAWARE	Peach blossom	Blue Hen Chicken
FLORIDA	Orange blossom	Mockingbird
GEORGIA	Cherokee rose	Brown Thrasher
HAWAII	Hawaiian hibiscus	Nene
IDAHO	Syringa, mock orange	Mountain Bluebird
ILLINOIS	Violet	Cardinal
INDIANA	Peony	Cardinal
IOWA	Wild prairie rose	Eastern Goldfinch
KANSAS	Sunflower	Western Meadowlark
KENTUCKY	Goldenrod	Cardinal
LOUISIANA	Magnolia	Eastern Brown Pelican
MAINE	White pine cone and tassel	Chickadee
MARYLAND	Black-eyed susan	Baltimore Oriole
MASSACHUSETTS	Mayflower	Chickadee
MICHIGAN	Apple blossom	Robin
MINNESOTA	Pink and white lady's slipper	Common Loon
MISSISSIPPI	Magnolia	Mockingbird
MISSOURI	Hawthorn	Bluebird
MONTANA	Bitterroot	Western Meadowlark
NEBRASKA	Goldenrod	Western Meadowlark
NEVADA	Sagebrush	Mountain Bluebird
NEW HAMPSHIRE	Purple lilac	Purple Finch
NEW JERSEY	Violet	Eastern Goldfinch
NEW MEXICO	Yucca flower	Roadrunner
NEW YORK	Rose	Bluebird
NORTH CAROLINA	Flowering dogwood	Cardinal
NORTH DAKOTA	Wild prairie rose	Western Meadowlark
OHIO	Scarlet carnation	Cardinal
OKLAHOMA	Oklahoma rose	Scissor-tailed Flycatcher
OREGON	Oregon grape	Western Meadowlark
PENNSYLVANIA	Mountain laurel	Ruffed Grouse
RHODE ISLAND	Violet	Rhode Island Red
SOUTH CAROLINA	Yellow jessamine	Great Carolina Wren
SOUTH DAKOTA	Pasque flower	Ring-necked Pheasant
TENNESSEE	Iris	Mockingbird
TEXAS	Bluebonnet	Mockingbird
UTAH	Sego lily	Common American Gull
VERMONT	Red clover	Hermit Thrush
VIRGINIA	American dogwood	Cardinal
WASHINGTON	Coast rhododendron	Willow Goldfinch
WEST VIRGINIA	Rhododendron	Cardinal
WISCONSIN	Wood violet	Robin
WYOMING	Indian paintbrush	Western Meadowlark

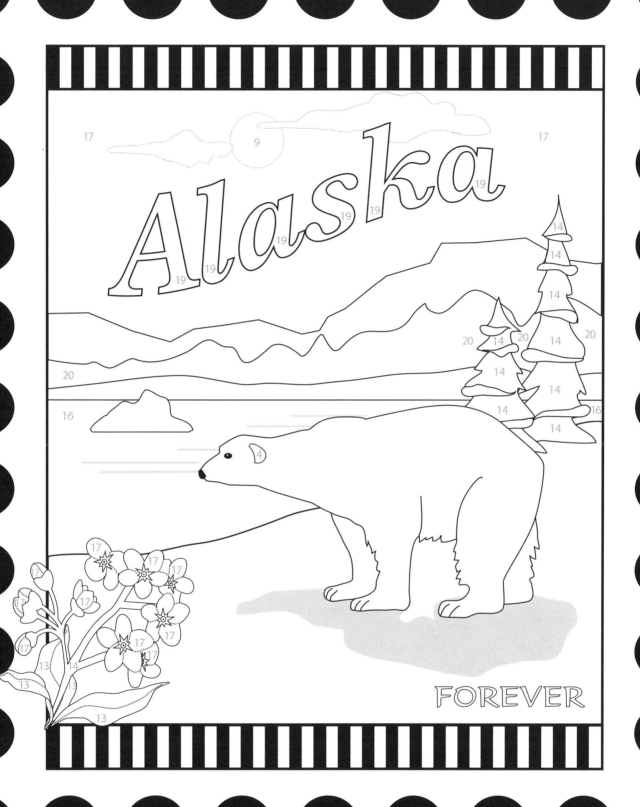

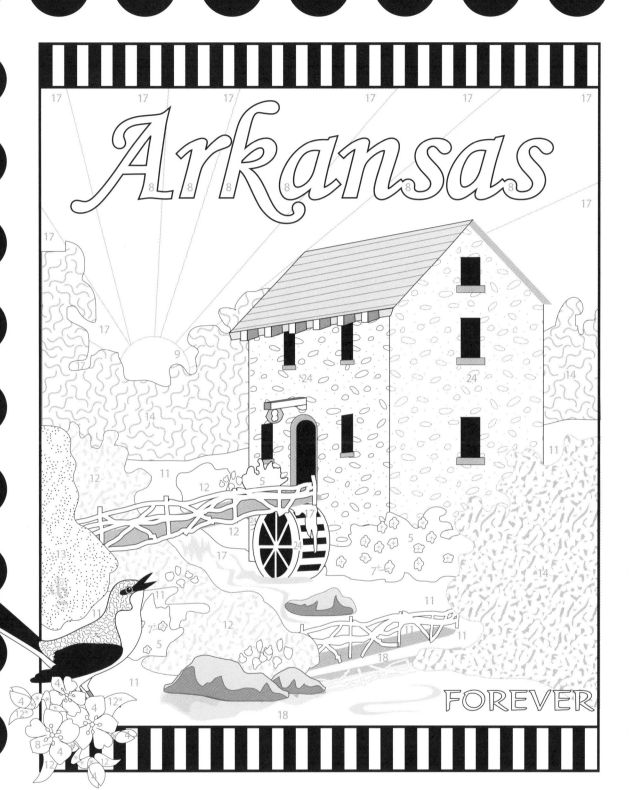

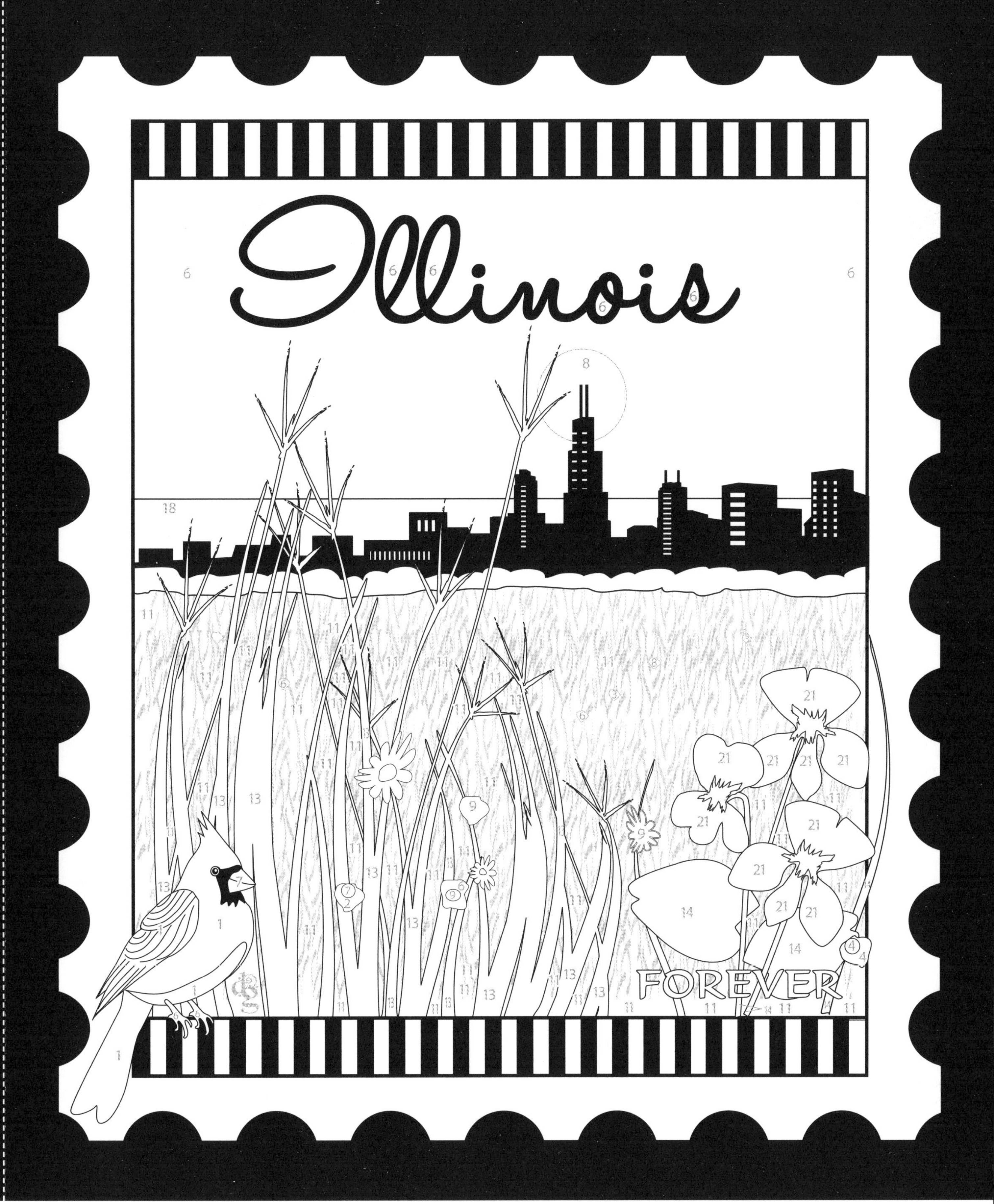
Illinois
FOREVER

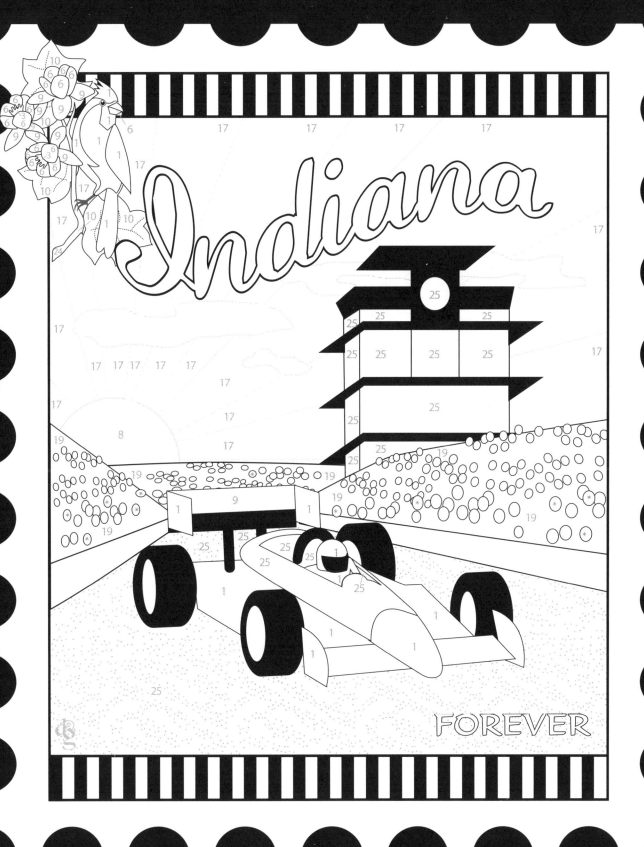

Indiana

FOREVER

* Dots in stands are multi-colored.

* Dots in stands are multi-colored.

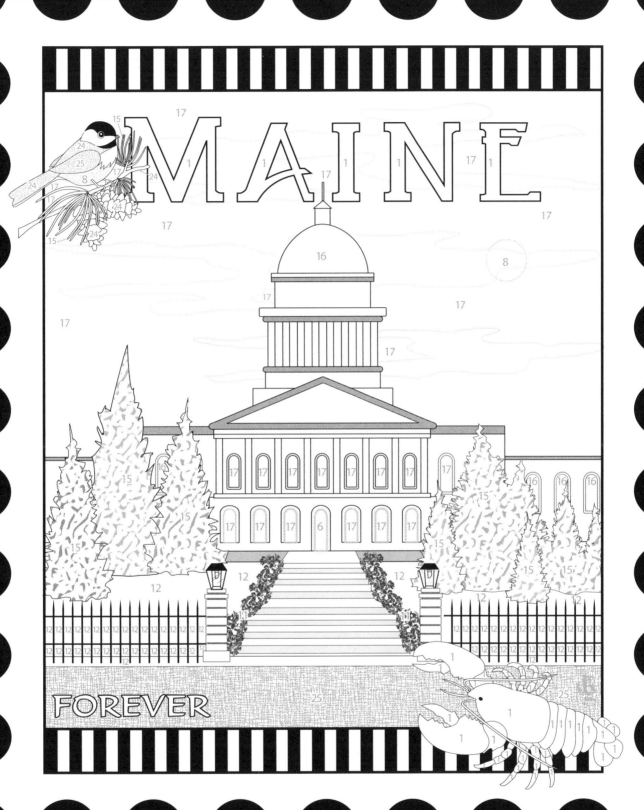

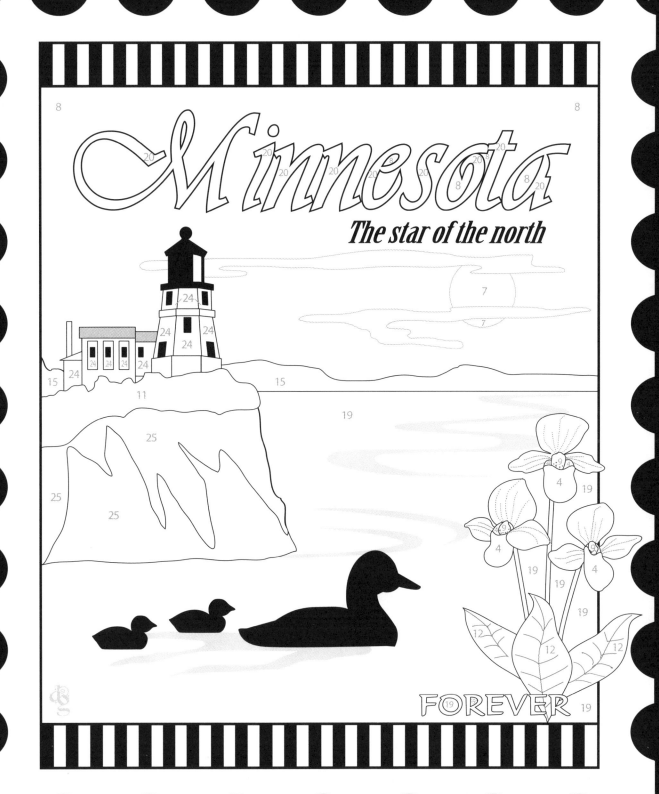

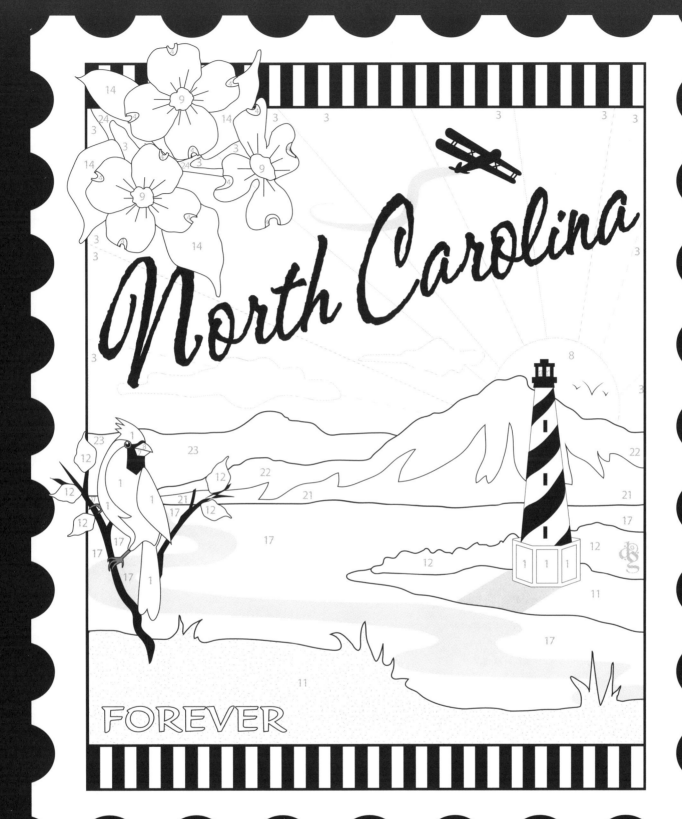

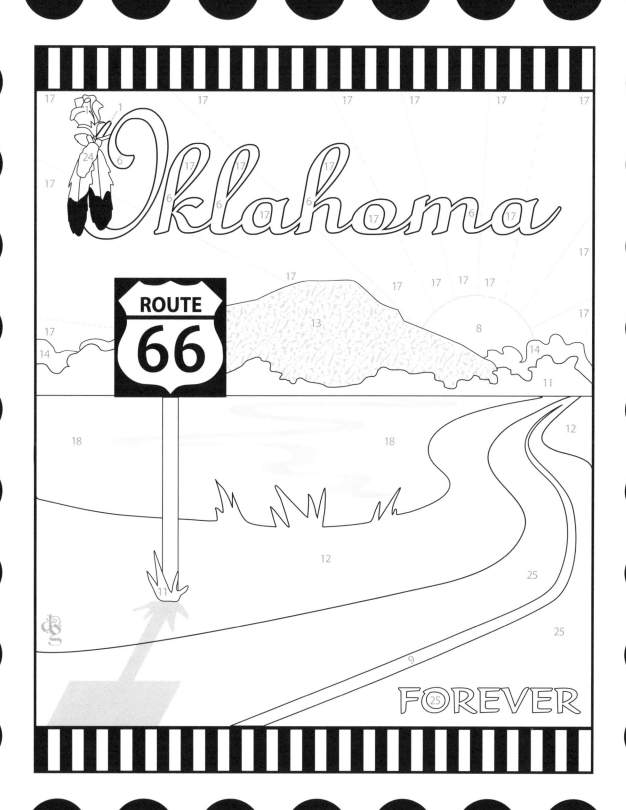

OREGON

FOREVER

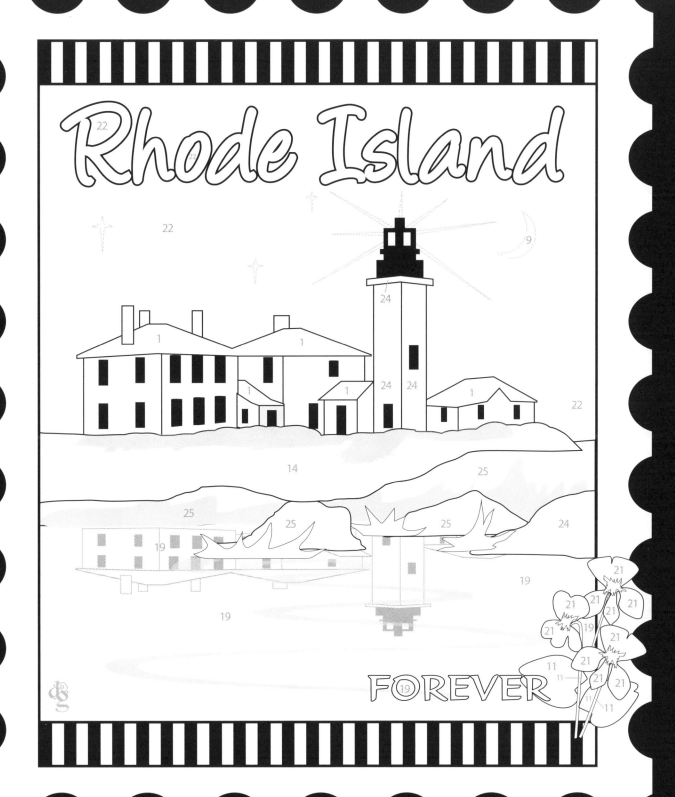

Yellowstone

National Park • Wyoming

Prismatic Spring

FOREVER